THE LIGHT IS STILL

*Correspondence between
Eugene Canadé and William Bronk*

Art by Eugene Canadé

W. Sheldon Hurst, Series Editor

VISUAL ARTS GALLERY
SUNY ADIRONDACK

EXHIBITION

THE LIGHT IS STILL

April 1 - 22, 2010

Visual Arts Gallery
SUNY Adirondack
Queensbury, New York

This book is not for sale and is to be distributed free of cost, thanks
to a grant from the Kingsbury Baptist Church Art Fund through the
SUNY Adirondack ACC Foundation, and a generous gift from The Hill Collection.

Published by SUNY Adirondack, Bay Road, Queensbury, NY 12804
Permission granted by The Trustees of Columbia University in the
City of New York to print the letters found in the William Bronk Papers,
Rare Book and Manuscript Library, Columbia University.

Book design by Susan Pearce.
Photographs of Canadé art by Stock Studio Photography and by Liz Lajeunesse.

COVER: Eugene Canadé, American, 1914-2001, *Shell Composition #1,* 1978,
Etching, 8/35, 2 7/8 x 1 7/8 WB. 1999.75

ACKNOWLEDGMENTS

This book is the result of the tremendous assistance of the librarians at Columbia University Rare Books and Manuscript Library in NYC, and I have appreciated their attention to the details. It has been a delight to work with Francesca Canadé Sautman, daughter of Eugene Canadé, who was most helpful in gathering the biography, bibliography and photographs of her father. I am grateful to Gloria Weil for providing photographs of her husband, Jim Weil. It was a joy to receive Daniel Leary's gift to the college of his series of photographs of Bill Bronk from that fall day in 1981. And I am grateful to Richard Carella for his advice and guidance throughout the planning of this book and the exhibition. His contribution of the autographed books for display makes an amazing tribute to all involved in the publications of poetry by William Bronk and illustrations by Eugene Canadé.

There would be no book without the generous assistance of Karen Hurst in transcribing the manuscripts of each letter by Bronk and Canadé. Ginevra Fisk, our student assistant, did a number of small projects that added up to very important contribution to the whole; this included identifying and editing the collection of photographs of Canadé's art in the SUNY Adirondack Art Collection. Thanks also to her and to Grace Ross for work done to install the exhibition in the gallery.

This is the eighth book in the SUNY Adirondack Art and Poetry series, and Susan Pearce has designed each with a sense of commitment that has made every one a beautiful, readable tribute to the creative work of those included in the exhibits and publications. She is a great asset to the work of the Visual Arts Gallery and to SUNY Adirondack.

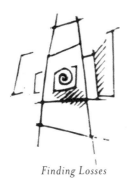

Finding Losses

Canadé's studio in Paris

BOOK, ART, LETTERS

Things of the present reflect the presence's light.
When the present is past and dark the light is still.

"LIGHT" BY WILLIAM BRONK[1]

There comes a time when looking back allows us to realize that the past can cast light into the present. This is such an occasion. Just over ten years ago, William Bronk died; almost ten years ago, Eugene Canadé died. The lives of two creative men are over: there are no more new Bronk poems, and new visual images will no longer come forth from the hand of Canadé. But in our looking back we know that there is still light. The work of Bronk and Canadé continues to be part of our lives, and in particular the books they worked on together continue to inspire. It is with this great awareness that the Visual Arts Gallery of SUNY Adirondack celebrates their friendship and collaboration.

Eugene Canadé, artist

William Bronk, poet

Bill and Eugene met at Cummington School for the Arts in 1938 when they were both young men. They had graduated from their respective colleges and were committed to lives of creative expression. The enduring friendship which began during that summer gathering of men and women from around the country continued for over sixty years, expressed in letters, visits, appreciation and sharing of one another's creative spirit and work, and in publications of Bill's poems which included Eugene's images.

5

SUNY Adirondack is pleased to play a role in casting light on this legacy, for it has become a part of ours as well; Bill bequeathed his art to the college at his death in 1999, and among the approximately 150 pieces were drawings, paintings, and prints by his friend Eugene. This example of friendship and gift of art has been the foundation of a college collection which has grown to over 700 pieces and is in evidence throughout the campus.

I first met Bill in 1985, at a dinner theater where by chance we shared a table. I was new to the area, and when he introduced himself I recognized his name and asked him if he was indeed the poet. He was, we talked, and he invited me to visit. I accepted, went home to read his award-winning *Life Supports*, made my first journey to his Hudson Falls home, and began a valued friendship that lasted until his death.

During that first visit to Bill's home, I took note of his collection of art. The walls carefully displayed paintings and prints by artists, most of whom were his personal friends. He noted my interest, and in subsequent meetings helped me to become acquainted with each piece, first by accompanying me on personal tours and later on by letting me explore on my own, and always by engaging in a discussion of the art as we sat together on the sun porch.

Eugene Canadé figured prominently in the collection. There were etchings of shell images that followed the stairs to the top floor; above his desk, a poster announced a 1963 exhibition of Eugene's work in Paris; paintings hung in various locations in the house. Most of the small prints of landscapes, cityscapes, still-life studies, and resting figures remained in the envelopes in which they had arrived with letters from Eugene, ready to show during a visit.

Bill gave me Eugene's Rue Pascal address in Paris prior to one of my visits there, and I was grateful for the opportunity to have my first encounter with this significant person in Bill's life. Eugene's studio was full of the finished, unfinished, not-yet-started but conceived and imagined work of a man whose life was spent creating. I had known the Cubist mural study that Bill had, but now I got to see a much larger one that hung above Eugene's studio desk. Images I had grown to know and appreciate back in the Hudson Falls home on Pearl Street I was now privileged to experience in other forms and in another space. His atelier and work confirmed the man whose art had so intrigued me.

James Weil, publisher

The graciousness with which Eugene welcomed and shared time with me was an indication of the kind of person William Bronk's friend was. A life-time of work with UNICEF attested to his commitment to a role in the larger world and to his concern with the issues of promoting relationships, communication, and diversity. His attention to me gave evidence of willingness to be present with a stranger: I was his guest in his home and at his favorite restaurant, and we talked late into the evening. The privilege was one that made me realize the depth of character of Eugene as well as the nature of the friendship claimed by Bill and Eugene.

It is these two men of the arts whose work together we are highlighting with this book and its concurrent exhibition. The first volume of Bill's poems that included Eugene's art was *Light and Dark*, published in the 1950s by Cid Corman; the book's cover design was by Eugene. In 1975, they began working with James Weil, publisher of The Elizabeth Press. Their first collaboration was a re-issue of *Light and Dark*, with Bill's poems and Eugene's images. The next year Eugene contributed woodcuts for the publication of Bill's *Finding Losses*. In 1979 they collaborated in *Force of Desire*. The high point in their united ventures came with the publication of Bill's *Life Supports*. It was printed in 1981 by The Elizabeth Press and followed by the North Point Press publication in 1981 and 1982. Bill received the National Book Award for Poetry for this work, for which Eugene provided woodcuts.

We are grateful to Richard Carella, Bill's friend for many years, for making available for exhibition a collection that includes a copy of each book that Bill and Eugene worked on together. Of particular note is a first edition of *Life Supports*, signed by both Bill and Eugene as well as by the publisher, Jim Weil, and by the designers, Giovanni and Martino Mardersteig.

We are also pleased to include in the exhibition photographs by Daniel Leary taken during these same years of the Bronk-Canadé collaboration. "A Walk with Bill" highlights Bill's frequent walks along the Hudson River feeder canal near his home.

Giovanni Mardersteig,
book designer

Martino Mardersteig,
book designer

The letters from which excerpts were taken for this book are housed at the Rare Book and Manuscript Library at Columbia University, where both Eugene and Bill had given their correspondence. A few years after both men had died, "when the present is past and dark," I made my way there. It was with great interest that I had the opportunity to read the letters they had exchanged during the 60 years of their friendship, beginning at Cummington and ending with Bill's death. It became apparent to me that I needed to celebrate the creative friendship of these two men, and this book and exhibition are the result. "The light is still"; Bill and Eugene have both died. "The light is still"; their poetry and art continue.

The planning of the exhibition of Eugene's art has been a great pleasure. All of Bill's extensive collection of Eugene's art—part of the poet's original gift to the college—is included. In addition, we are indebted to Eugene's daughter, Francesca Canadé Sautman, for loaning us a fine selection of sketches, drawings, prints and paintings from her personal collection. These works help to illuminate the artist's working style and point to the diverse interests he had throughout his life.

The book, the art, the letters: these are evidence of the continuing light that we can experience, thanks to the friendship of Eugene Canadé and William Bronk. Our gratitude recognizes that "the light is still."

— W. Sheldon Hurst

[1] Bronk, William. "Light" in *Living Instead*. San Francisco: North Point Press, 1991, page 91.

Correspondence between
Eugene Canadé and William Bronk

Art by Eugene Canadé

Bridge at Night

Dear Gene,

Cid Corman who is the editor of a little magazine called *Origin* that I have been appearing in—you may have seen a copy or so I don't remember—is now in Italy and wants to have printed there a little collection of some of my poems. He suggested a facsimile manuscript or a drawing for a cover design. I would rather have a drawing. Would you be willing to do something? I think I may use *Light and Dark* for a title (from the poem Winterberry Song which you may remember from one of my Christmas cards though that poem may not appear in the collection) but the drawing need not illustrate anything. I think we see with eyes enough alike so that anything you might do would be harmonious with the contents. And supposing it weren't? No matter. Size of the book—5 x 7. If you like the idea maybe it would be a good idea to find out from Corman what he could reproduce adequately. Or maybe you know anyway....

Well, I have had a productive summer. After an essay on time and the Mayas which somehow failed to function I wrote a series of poems using some of the same themes. They worked out pretty well although the last two or three don't excite me much. The man who has charge of the poetry room at Widener Library at Harvard asked me for some manuscripts and I went on display there today when school started. I suppose I did. That was the schedule. There is some fun in the idea of the book and the exhibit but I hope both ventures flop. It would be awful to *arrive*. I would have to admit I hadn't been there all along. And I could easily get so excited about it that it would be an additional excuse for not working. I have wondered how much of my burst of activity this summer was a result of really low spirits about my failure to get any place or produce anything and the rushing decline of business. So now both conditions have quite reversed themselves. And I may do nothing. It is better to work secretly and in the dark like those djinns in the Arabian Nights who built palaces all fountains and precious stones between sunset and sunrise even if the work is done in what feels like despair (which may indeed be the secret condition).

I envy Ethel Mt. St. Michel.

My best to all

B

Cityscape

Dear Bill,

I have been trying to write to you for the last three days to tell you that I'd love to do the drawing for your book. I am also very glad for you that you are going to have something published.

Your friend Corman and I have been in correspondence already although our letters crossed. I have asked him some questions (just like an expert which I certainly no longer am) and I hope I can do something good for you. Thanks for your confidence in me. I would much rather have been able to send you several tries for you to select or reject. I no longer am so good and I guess I am gradually petrifying or is that the word. I am losing contact with all I think I love and rarely have even the consolation of a lively discussion. Anyhow I'll give it a whish and hope for the best. I would so much have liked it to be something really good.

Corman tells me I have something less than two weeks to get the job done. So far I haven't got any idea of what will appear in the book, how he plans to place the type on the cover, what kind of type and in fact what kind of cover.

The next time you get yourself published I hope you have someone who doesn't work at lightning speed. Then perhaps we can work out something really good. Don't think I am really complaining and that I find it difficult to do this job. You can't imagine what a pleasure it gave me and how it revived old unused instincts just to think about it. I only find it illogical that a publisher would expect a man to design a cover or a page or what have you without giving you the basic elements. A drawing for reproduction must be conceived in relation to the paper on which it is printed (or rather surface). It is not possible to print every drawing in any kind of surface and expect good results.

Anyway I am having fun at it and it has given me a new surge of energy to begin again looking for a Paris residence for you (I have so far been miserably unsuccessful and discouraged). I'll try to send you a copy of some sort of whatever I produce so you can see what it is and stop press if not suitable.

Ethel and kids send their best wishes.

Gene

For the Canadés of Paris VIII

I am told you already have five (5) copies so you get this poem on a plain sheet of paper rather than on the flyleaf of *Light and Dark* as ordinary non-contributing people are getting it. I like the cover drawing better than I had expected to like it though I guess I still prefer the other design that Corman characterized as too static for my poetry. His printing job is a cramped and smudgy scramble, isn't it? Well OK, no matter. In October, I went to Boston where I was having a manuscript show at the Harvard Library poetry room and was hustled to a studio to make a recording. *That* was a shock to me when I heard it and I think maybe I show to better advantage in smeared little type than I do in the sound of my own voice—if that was my own voice and I'm not fully convinced it was. They put in a ringer on me I think—maybe a dead-ringer—or so it sounded. Or they used the auditory equivalent of fun house mirrors. But since we do have to live with ourselves, with our own faces, voices, smells, etc., no doubt it may be as well to know just how much we are up against.

Bonne année à tout le monde Canadé

B

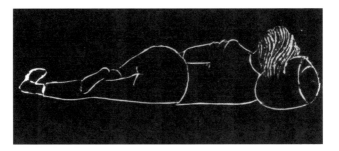

Reclining Figure

Virgin and Child with Music and Numbers

Who knows better than you know
Lady, the circumstances of this event
—meanness, the overhanging terror and the need
for flight soon—hardly reflect the pledge
the angel gave you, the songs you exchanged in joy
with Elizabeth, your cousin? That was then
or that was for later, another time. Now—

Still the singing was and is. Song
whether or not we sing. The song is sung.
Are we cozened? The song we hear is like
those numbers we cannot factor whose overplus,
an indeterminate fraction, seems more than the part
we factor out. Lady, if our despair
is to be unable to factor ourselves in song
or factor the world there, what should our joy
be other than that same integer that sings
and mocks at satisfaction? We are not
fulfilled. We cannot hope to be. No,
we are held, somewhere in the void of whole despair,
enraptured; and only there does the world endure.

Lady, sing to this Baby, even so.

Dear Ethel,

The day for pinning-on fishes. Gray and chilly here though not scouring cold wind of the last few days and the only connection with fishes is that today the trout season opens….

I'm glad you saw the review by way of Hinch. In the other direction it got as far as Denver where Al Pew saw it. Herman Maril called me Sunday from Baltimore. His copy of the *Times* for that Sunday never reached him but his son had just called from Worcester Massachusetts (2 weeks later?) to say he had seen it and would send it to Herman.

Jim Weil is reissuing *Light and Dark* which hasn't been available for several years. It will come out later this year (or early next?) along with *Silence and Metaphor* which are the eight-liners. I remembered that Gene had done several drawings for *L & D* and that the one Corman used was not the one Gene liked. So I dug way back and found the others and Jim will use the better one this time. It should be a much more elegant book.

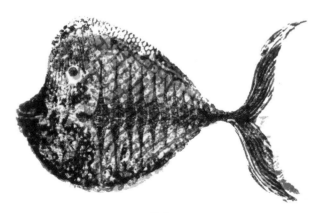

Fish

Here are some samples of the 4-liners.

He Praises Nescience and Impotence

1. Whoever's in charge's in charge the same way
we are: there are things we can do
and things we can't do. We make a try.
We are whatever there is whatever we are.

2. Blessed art thou, o God, in thy impotence.
If there is another way to live as we wish
there were we would. What more were there?
Love God. We are at one in this.

The World

I thought that you were an anchor in the drift of the world;
but no: there isn't an anchor anywhere.
There isn't an anchor in the drift of the world. Oh no.
I thought you were. Oh no: The drift of the world.

Like an Island Downriver from Us

What we call love is a safe place before
we get to desire. It has its own perils;
but we stop off there and play with desire
knowing how it will destroy us utterly. [2]

Love to you both
    B

---

[2] Poems are selected from those included in the letter.

Dear Gene and Ethel,

I was pleased to have Gene's letter and to learn that the studio was workable and worked in again. Even I have been working a little. Jim Weil was here last week and I gave him a collection of the 4-liners to publish. That will be for 76 when he will also do my first collection which was never published—things I wrote when we first knew each other—at Cummington and NY and the time in HF before the war and during the war. He will also do a little book—a few things I wrote between the end of the eight-liners *(Silence and Metaphor,* which will be out in the fall) and the 4-liners I just gave him.

Also in the fall—November—there will be something like a group show in the arcade of City University on 42nd between 5th and 6th—across from the back corner of the Library. Some organization which I think is the same one that puts the big pieces of sculpture around on the streets in NY is sponsoring something called Poetry in Public Places. They mean to print poems on 4'0 x 8'0 placards and display them, have noontime readings, offer the poems also in broadside and portfolio and send the show on tour. They took 5 of my 4-liners. I think it should be fun. Kind of a carnival sideshow.

When Jim Weil was here he brought a proof of the drawing for *Light and Dark* and I thought it looked very good.

Here are some of the concluding poems of the 4-liner collection. I call it *Finding Losses.*

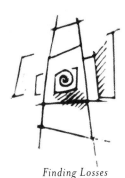

Finding Losses

External Determinants

All the mechanisms of the body—the forced
flow of the blood, for example, seem more complex
than what the body may accomplish with them
if it ever does. Our forms are not our forms.

Surprise Ending

Of course, in a sense, we aren't anyone.
No, more than a sense. But there isn't someone across
the galaxy either, or no one we could talk
to, ever. Oddly, talk is what it's about.

The Inability

She wants me to say something pretty to her because
we both know the unabettable
bleak of the world. Make believe, she says,
What harm? It may be so. I can't. I don't.

The Pardon

If there were a maker I'd praise the maker but
I think there isn't one; making is ours.
My random love sings at random. I
(who am I?) sing nevertheless (to what?): I praise.

Friendly Greeting

All love is self-love; the other is not.
It is ourselves we particle.
Love has to have something. There is nothing more.
Hello, we say, I have been waiting for you.[3]

Love to you both
   B

---

[3] Poems are selected from those included in the letter.

Dear Gene and Ethel,

Well you aren't as bad as I Gene. I have still your July letter unanswered and here now is another. I hope you are keeping track of the checks. I haven't; but you must have come close to the end if you haven't passed it already. The last one came timely for a novelist and a sculptor in straits. The fund revolves.

Jim Weil called me. He was very pleased with the printing job Mardersteig had done on the *L and D* drawing. He had an unbound copy from him by air. So the books should be bound and shipped in a month or two. When Jim comes here in October I'll suggest to him that we might do a book together as you were thinking of last summer and see how he responds....

Corman's anthology from the old issues of ORIGIN was advertised in the New York Review of Books this week. I am the biggest contributor to it. A woman called me last week about a reading in New York this winter—but I had the feeling she was using me and was indignant and I guess I shouted at her. As the years go on I get closer to what I remember of Pop's bitterness and anger. I hope I develop some of the sweetness he still had with it all. But the whole experience gets more and more mysterious and incredible to me. Coming home from Laura's Sunday just before dawn the old bright winter stars were in the sky and Venus had just come up in the east as big and bright almost as a sun in the blackness. It is true our experience is mundane but our monde is in the stars, the middle of the heavens.

Galaxy

The Insufficiency

Night and day, the seasons, are as if someone
had arranged them. They were never arranged.
Oh, how marvelous the world is
and I without the strength sometimes to know.

The Things that Are Are Not

Order is what teaches us the abstract because
whatever we make of order defaults, is wrong.
Things and systems all come apart. There is no
order we can live with. There is nothing else.

What We Call Force. Gravity?

Thinking of you as something (someone) is my
error; but that's a laugh too: who am I?
All right. I put it all on you. Or it went
there. Galaxies form like that.

What It Is

The excitement from people seems to be from themselves
though we know it is not. Seeing the light on trees,
especially in summer—oh, beautiful then
we know it to be the light and not the trees.

Ignorance

I am concerned about our deaths as we all are.
There may be a real world (as I think there is)
of which we know as little as we do of our lives.
We don't know our deaths are not in that world.[4]

My love to you both
    B

---

[4] Poems are selected from those included in the letter.

Steeple

Dear Bill,

I have been trying to get a letter off to you for several days but have not had a single free moment. As you see, I am back in Lugano unexpectedly. My brother-in-law, Carl Zigrosser, died suddenly last week and I had to rush here to be with Laura. I shall be here until the end of next week and shall probably arrive in New York the following week.

Since I was in the area and as a good excuse to take Laura away from her apartment for a bit, I made a trip to Verona last Wednesday and saw Mardersteig, the younger.

We had a good hour together and agreed on a number of possible things. In brief, he'd even prefer to print from woodcuts or linoleum cuts. No problem with a run of 400 copies. If I do the cuts he will make a few copies at the beginning of the run on special paper. These will serve to make plates in the event—a) of an accident to the original cuts during or before printing is completed and b) for any reprinting which may be done at a later date.

Mardersteig is printing 4 pages up and while he can fit in six illustrations it would be easier for him to work with four or eight. In any case, he suggests that I do nothing definite until he provides a first proof which he thinks will be sometime during the latter part of January. He will send me a set directly to Paris. That's a good idea because he can then indicate the beginning of each signature which may be the best place of each illustration and having the proofs will give some idea of the general tone of his pages of text.

He says that he will in any event run the illustrations separate from the text. He also suggested that if we want to use color one or two colors will not increase the cost. I said that would be a matter for Weil to decide. Color is not necessary but we could think of it.

If I can produce the blocks, either wood or lino, our first edition would be with original engravings and that would be quite a nice idea.

If you are talking to Weil, would you mind communicating the above? I doubt I shall be able to steal more time to write separately. I'll let you know when I expect to be in NY.

As ever,

Gene

Dear Gene,

I have the proofs this morning and better get a reply right back to you the mails being now so slow. So far so good. I only wish there were more but I realized when I read the poems to you in HF that I was asking for something almost hopeless. It is quite true those poems just don't leave openings. They are hermetic and forbidding. Bravo for managing to wedge in four. They will certainly add materially to the collection and perhaps open it out a little. I am especially excited by the voluptuous embrace and its tight sinuosity.

I called Jim and reported to him. I'm sure you and Martino Mardersteig will work out the layout successfully.

Laura and I drove to Montreal last Monday and back on Tuesday…. A beautiful drive through the mountains, both days clear.

Springish days at last and the snow mostly gone and the snowdrops and crocus beginning to blossom….

My gratitude to you and my love to you and Laura both.

B

Paysage

Dear Bill,

I'm stopping over in Geneva for a couple of days to see a few Unicef colleagues and friends before returning to Paris. I finished my tasks in Lugano and have Laura reasonably settled in a new apartment. She and I went to Verona on Monday.

I delivered four blocks to MM [Martino Mardersteig]. He ran off a first proof from which I made a few corrections. The second and final proof seemed good to me so we agreed on it and I asked him to mail copies to you. I did not have a chance to send you a rough proof of the fourth block.

We could not agree completely on the placement of the illustrations. My own idea was to place them at the side and bottom of the pages I indicated. I must confess that even in final proof they do seem too dominant. We discussed these possibilities: 1) using my idea of placement at bottom of pages but printed in a grey silk. 2) printing in black on insert pages of the same color as the cover (MM's suggestion) and 3) printing in black on white paper same stock as text but on separate pages. Of ideas 2 and 3, 2 may be the best. However, for the moment I prefer no. 1.

MM will run off proofs in grey on white and black on colored stock. We should receive copies. He will discuss with Jim who is visiting him this or next week.

I shall be in New York on 19 April and we can discuss with Jim and agree which of the solutions we prefer.

I received your last letter in Lugano. I am sorry to have disappointed you by producing so few illustrations. Unfortunately, so many other things happened at the same time that I did not have enough time to think and work out more and the three weeks I had seemed really to pass so quickly. Perhaps on the next book we can have more time to work.

Aff.

Gene

Dear Gene,

Thanks for the proofs including the new one which I like very much. Jim is in Verona now.

I'll be reading (with a young friend) in NY on 17 May (Monday) at 8:00 PM CUNY Graduate Center on 42nd between 5th and 6th 8th floor.

Here is a little poem meanwhile

First, is to learn we have no strength of our own.
Second, an outside power is impotent, too.
The strength we acquire is to live with powerlessness.

Love
B

Still Life with Eggplants

The light can come through you; not that you
matter. But the light does. Why should you
twist, then, and turn, hiding it?

I can be glad in my death that, selfless,
the beauty of the world goes on; and then more:
even worldless, that beauty still.

The poem is momentary though it has not
the same moment always; changes occur
and it changes with them. Its moment is felt.[5]

Dear Gene and Ethel,

These are the ones subsequent to the tape which you have and I may
have repeated some. Rather that than omit.

Very pleased to hear that you have been painting, Gene. And to have
your lovely poem, Ethel.

Jim Weil called me this morning with the figures from the distribution
according to which I sold 500 copies of the various books last year. This
doesn't make me a best-seller but I was pleased at that number.

I have always been a winter-hater but I'm not really minding this one.
The cold is pretty steady but we have many bright sunny days.

Love

B

[5] Poems are selected from those included in the letter.

Queensboro Bridge No. 2

Dear Gene,

Thank you for the nice print in the mail today. If that was the reject for Jim's book the other must be very fine or else it was a hard choice. I would have been reluctant to reject this one. How are you coming with *The Force of Desire*. I hope it is not so abstract as to defeat you entirely.

I haven't really written anything since I finished that collection. One day follows another and I don't do much but keep, as they say, house and go to, as they say, business. The latter is now advertised for sale—whatever that may mean and I think not much.

Some of the garden is planted and I hope to get around to the rest of it this week or on the long weekend coming up. Mother came home a week ago and seems in very good shape for 89. She tires easily but then—so do I.

I had, surprisingly, a very sensitive and sympathetic review in the *Dartmouth Alumni Magazine* and there is supposed to be one coming up in the Sunday *Times*. *Finding Losses* is 2/3 or more gone and Jim is getting ready for an offset reprint. Otherwise, not much.

Love to you both

B

Dear Bill,

I've been meaning to write for what seems like months but my letter writing deteriorates if possible. For one thing Jim Weil is the most prolific letter writer and keeps me busy answering his voluminous correspondence.

I am so happy to hear that *Finding Losses* is doing so well and hope that if Jim goes into a second edition it will make out even better. As far as *Force of Desire* is concerned I've not yet put anything down on paper but continue to listen to the tape and should soon start committing myself.

I learn from Jim that you are now aware of his efforts to assist me in the Force of Desire project. I didn't want to involve you in that. Jim's [tactic was to try] to make suggestions and it took me a while to find a delicate way to make him understand that I couldn't work that way. He was quite nice about it and we finally agreed that it would be fine if he wanted to comment on your work and so incite me. I have now received his "hand hold" as he calls it and which he apparently discussed with you. I must confess that after having read it several times I find it difficult to understand and that I get much more "feeling" from the poems themselves.

I'm glad you liked the cut I sent. Jim just sent me a few copies of the final printing of his poem and the cut he selected. I personally prefer the art he selected and think the young lady who did the printing did a very good job. I hope Jim sends you a copy, if not let me know and I'll send you one from here.

In February I decided to start doing some etchings. I had an awful lot of trouble for a month or so relearning the process which I haven't used since '38 or '39. I finally succeeded in mastering the basic technique and have now finished with reasonable success six small etchings. I've only run trial and final proofs. As soon as I find the proper ingredients for making a good etching ink I'll run the final editions and will send you the prints.

I've had several interesting times and so work has been a little irregular. Last night Laura arrived from Lugano and I am sure I'll not have much—if any—time to work for another week or so. I also had an offer of a job in Geneva which I accepted since it would have helped the treasury a bit and so stopped work in preparation for a hurried departure for Geneva.

Finding Losses

The job fell through finally so I'll not be gainfully employed and lost practically two weeks of work. I've in preparation three drawings for somewhat larger etching plates but have no idea when I can get to do them. In the meantime I'll probably continue the series of small plates which should end up with about 12, all shell compositions.

Not counting possible employment, I've a pretty ambitious programme and hope to be able to tackle it quickly. Apart from a cut for Jim for a book he's now preparing and the cuts for *Force of Desire* I'd like to get enough work together to have an exhibition next year. This would include paintings, etchings, and a series of sculptures I've wanted to do for some years.

Is there any chance of your changing your mind about traveling to Europe? We'd love to have you here. I'd half hoped my NY colleagues would come through with another assignment in NY but I have not had any sign of life from them....

Love,

Gene

Dear Gene,

Jim was here a couple of weeks ago and brought me a copy of *To Her Hand*. I thought the cut you ended up using was beautiful and, to my mind, much the better of the two. Interesting to hear about your adventures with the etchings and I look forward to seeing the series when you finish with them.

Jim's "handhold" seemed to me to be a probably legitimate reading of *The Force of Desire* but one that I hadn't quite expected. I suggest you might be as well off to just go on your own reading and not be swayed by his. You said at one point that the poems didn't lend themselves to representational cuts and you thought that the best or anyway final solution would be abstracts that corresponded in feeling with the poems. To me, this would be a very good way to approach it. If it still seems a good idea to you—why don't you do that? But you know anything you want to do is OK with me.

Love to you both and to Laura

B

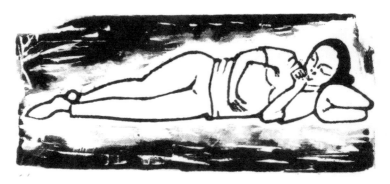

Sleeping Girl

Dear Gene,

I am delighted with the new etchings in such a way that it is hard for me to prefer one against another so I told Jim I would leave the choice to him—whatever would seem to work best with the production. Giovanni Mardersteig's obituary was in the *Times* one day last week and a day or so later a piece about the Officino and the probability that it would continue. Jim says there are other high quality shops in Verona and that it is Martino's intention to pick up a couple of pressions from them and to continue the Officino as a printing but not as a publishing house.

I spent the ten days before and including Christmas at Jane's and started off by sort of "officiating" at the marriage of a young friend at a farm house in southern Maryland. The bride and groom are both more or less Buddhists and wanted a home-made ceremony and I was it. It all went off well and I am thinking of putting a discrete and tasteful sign in the front yard "WEDDINGS." It's a big house and I could cater the reception on the premises.

Force should be a very beautiful book. One great pleasure I have in the etchings is in the continual insistence on their theme and subject through all its variations which is very much in consonance with the form and matter of the poems.

Love and bonne année to you all

And thanks for (among so many other things) the beautiful greeting for the New Year.

B

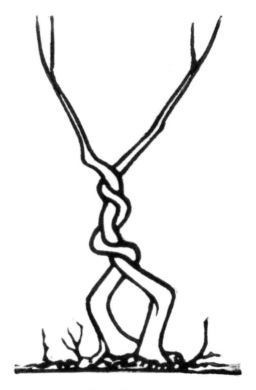

Winter Vocative

Dear Gene,

I have been sitting here looking through the poems to decide what I might read on the eleventh at Amherst. I think I'll do some little seasonal things first—late winter, early spring weather and landscapes—then some longer more intellectual pieces like the Anselm and the Canaletto and end with short personal lyrics. But, so often, I decide at the last minute to do something else besides what I had planned to do. I have another reading at Yale in April. Both of these were really arranged by Jim's initiative. Otherwise, I doubt if anyone would have asked me this year. A man at Dartmouth reported himself as planning to ask me but found too many impediments or perhaps never cared that much.

I have the photo of the long mural and the etchings through #11, and, of course, am very pleased, grateful and involved with them. The movement and the contemplation absorb me. I'd love to see the mural in the original in order to have a direct impression of its tones, from side to side.

Even if it is the first of March the winter cold continues. We should be having a few mild days but we aren't. Nevertheless, probably as defiance more than hope, I went through the catalog and ordered garden seed today. The garden is deep in snow.

I had a letter today from a young poet whom I don't know but who sent me his book which I liked very much and I wrote and told him so. He said it was my judgment he had waited for and my writing had been his touchstone ever since *The World the Worldless*. I guess this is better than being famous and selling widely.

Love to you both

B

Shell Composition #7

Dear Gene,

I read at the Yale Library last week. In "The Art of the Book Room" there was a big exhibit of the work of the two Mardersteigs and we were both included in the exhibit—you by the woodcut you did for *To Her Hand* and the one for *The World*. The reading was sparsely attended but I don't draw crowds anyway and I had a good time.

...Herman is getting a grant from the National Institute and Academy or however they call it—the one uptown in the same plaza with the Museum of the American Indian. The presentation is next month and they will be showing some of his paintings and he offered me an invitation but I told him someone else might enjoy it more....Well, I'm pleased for him if he's pleased but he doesn't need that academic nonsense and if it were me (as it is not likely it ever should be) I would just say no. I am lucky that I have never had to worry about the "success" of my work. Hardly anyone reads me or comes to hear me read and I go on writing whatever I get to write just as though there were thousands of readers waiting for it. Of course, I am also lucky to have Jim who is willing to publish whatever I give him even though he may never recover the cost of publication—or not for a long time anyway. All the books together and there must be ten or a dozen now hardly reach 4 or 5 hundred copies a year and it isn't just their cost. *The World the Worldless* is still available in paper for $1.50. It sold 15 copies in the first quarter of the year. So, all right, no matter.

The landscape is still grim and bleak though there is a little green in places and the snow is gone except for piles on the north side of houses. Crocus and snowdrops are blossoming. There is still frost some nights. I have some seeds planted but only in the house. Sorrel is coming up in the garden.

I'm glad the shell mural was pleasing. Judging from the photo, it certainly should have been.

Did I tell you that the little 3 liner about my zip code is displayed among the advertisements on the cards on the buses in cities of NYS this month? It's supposed to be anyway. I haven't heard from anybody who has seen it.

Next month Paul Auster has a piece about my work in the *Saturday Review*.

Love

  B

Dear Gene,

Your beautiful holiday card today with no accompanying note rebukes me for my own failure in not writing to you but I think of us as always in communication even in our silences. The Aquarius has such a tender lyrical grace it makes me happy to be in that sign myself (even though "in the cusp" as they say). The way the conventional sign echoes the undulations of the figure's outline and the long, forward thrust of the leg and trunk the force of the issuing water is magnificent.

We closed the office the first of October and I have had only occasional business chores since then. The real estate is still unsold and there are some collectibles to collect. The days go by almost unnoticed and I wonder sometimes at how much I haven't done. There were the leaves to rake, earlier, and the storm sash to put on so that one could think of something done; but now that the ground is snow-covered and no outside work to do and nothing done—a walk by the canal, bookshelves rearranged maybe—I wonder what I ever needed to do. Nothing much gets written either, though I wait for that. I attend on it. Well, patience, patience! People on the street ask what am I doing now and I tell them it doesn't take much to keep me busy. I thought I might read or reread some books but the occasion doesn't come, or is put off. When Betty and I went off on vacations I used to carry a number of books with me and usually brought them home again, unread. Someone calls on the phone or comes for a visit and the day is over, or the week….

I have the shell compositions hanging on the wall going up the front stairs where they do better than in a portfolio.

Laura and I went a month ago to Scranton where I did a reading. The only one scheduled this season until Middlebury in February. I did one last summer at Woodstock. Later in November we went to Boston where a man who teaches at New England Conservatory was presenting a musical piece based on texts from poetry including some of mine. It was interesting but so sophisticatedly modern that the text disappeared in the texture which may well have been the idea and no doubt a very good idea at that. Anyway, we had a good time.

Bridge #5

Jim Weil is coming to spend the day on the 15th. He wants to talk about the production of a collected poems and of the old *Brother in Elysium*, the Thoreau-Whitman-Melville book I worked on years ago at Cummington and here and in Hanover. I don't know when they may appear. Mardersteig seems so overloaded and behind schedule I have almost given up expecting *The Force of Desire*.

Love to you both
    B

Yellow Church

Dear Bill,

I spent the month of February in Rome working for that new UN organization. The last week there I caught a cold which developed into a flu and came back limp as a rag. I've been back in Paris for almost two weeks and still unable to shake the cold and this terrible feeling of weariness.

Yesterday, the enclosed letter came to me. I've, of course, kept all or most of your letters but it never occurred to me to sell them. I don't know what you would like me to do about it so before saying more to Mr. Miller than I am consulting you I'll wait for your reply. If you think it will help you to have some of these letters available to the people interested in you, I can send the whole lot to you so that you can select what you think is most appropriate. If not, I'll write to the fellow and tell him they are all personal letters and not for public consumption.

On my return from Rome, I found the colophones for signature (*Force*). I signed them and returned them to Mardersteig a day or so later. I trust he has received them by now. He's not one to write much so I may have to call him this week to check.

I've not heard from Weil in quite some time which is surprising since I don't know anyone who is so prompt and prolific in producing letters. He did speak in one of his more recent letters about more illustrations. As there was nothing definite in his letter I've done nothing about it. If anything is wanted let me know and I'll get to work.

With this temporary job for Rome my time has been pretty spotty. So I've done little work here at the studio and even my second big canvas is still unfinished. I've used the bits of time between visits to Rome to prepare canvases and materials. So I now have a studio full of nice blank white canvases and a new very big one. The accumulation of finished, started and unattacked canvases has invaded the studio so that I have less and less room. I am now constantly moving them to get at things I need.

I'll probably be going back to Rome in April again and so between feeling not that well and so little time ahead I've embarked on a series of etchings from a sketch of the Queensborough Bridge. None finished yet but perhaps this week I'll have a few "states" to see what I've managed to do so far….

Love,
Gene

Dear Gene,

…I am supposed to do a reading for Mannes College in April but the date hasn't been set so I don't know whether it may be while Ethel is there. The reading is a benefit with some musicians on the program also to make it possible to sell the tickets. The pending merger of Mannes and Manhattan was called off and Mannes needs money badly.

I don't see any advantage to me at all for Hugh Miller to have letters or papers of mine for sale. He has offered to buy things from me and he wrote to Elman. I don't know what others he may have written to. I may sell some manuscripts if I need the money as I get older though I don't want to sell anything now when I don't need to. I would trust your discretion entirely if you ever want to sell him something. I know you wouldn't let him have anything harmful. I don't even suppose you have anything that is.

Jim and I don't expect to see any copies of *The Force of Desire* before May or later. Mardersteig is coming to Jim's for a visit in April and we are hoping he may bring with him the proofs of *The Brother in Elysium* which he is supposed to have been setting but I am not at all counting on it. I think Mardersteig takes on too much work. But I suppose he is worth waiting for and we all know how long we wait for our own work. I have continued to work on the 20-line poems at an average rate of about one a month. That's 3 or 4 years to make a decent collection. But also I have lived long enough now to have accumulated, however slowly, a quantity of work. Not many people read it or even know about it. A few friends and other poets do and respect it and that's better in all ways than being famous.

Love

B

Dear Gene,

...I found the design of *Force* other than I expected but I got used to it and I was very pleased with your etchings in it. The book has had no impact or notice so far and probably won't have any. But then. Fortunately, I find it true that the work is its own reward. I guess you feel the same way.

The bridge pieces are impressively and movingly strong and I am very grateful for them. When I took them to the framer he convinced me that if, in matting them, he did not preserve the relation between the print itself and the size and shape of the paper it was printed on he would not be altering your intention. Later, I thought I had done wrong to be convinced. What say?

I continue with the 20-line poems which Jim plans to use as the last section of the *Collected Poems* in 1981 (?) I have a reading at Cooper Union on the 7th November....

Well, love to both of you

B

Trees

A WALK WITH BILL

from *One Day in the Fall of 1981*

PHOTOGRAPHS BY DANIEL LEARY

Down past the T

*Walking along
the Five Combine*

Harvesting wild grapes

At Sherman's Farm

Dear Gene and Ethel,

I dreamed about the Canadés last night and though the dream had the usual transpositions that dreams have—the quarters resembled nothing I remember and the only child in evidence was Laurie who was a six or seven year old boy—you were definitely there.

I should dream of you more often and might be a less dilatory correspondent. It's been a strange time: I haven't written anything for many months but begin now to get more invitations to read—including one this week to read at Amherst on behalf of Cummington. I was so annoyed at Cummington when I read there before that I may or may not do it. *The Force of Desire* has had no notice except in some bibliographical publication which didn't really approve of the design and felt it was wrong to print me in such an elegant typeface and, in that inequity the implied fault in measuring up was mine. Jim had a letter from Martino last week to say *The Brother in Elysium* was at the binders and would be shipped this month; but it will probably be as little noticed as *TFOD*. Well it's not a new experience.

The winter has been almost snowless and without any really cold temperatures and the winter landscape on my walks seems richly colored in its limited pallette. Blue, black grey and brown can have infinite values and depths and contrasts….

La Provincia di Genova is flying me over for a week in April with a group of other poets for some sort of US-Italy poetry gathering. We don't perform but listen to Italian critics comment on our work. Very strange, but why protest? It's a strange world anyway.

Love

B

Dear Bill,

If I've taken so long to write it's because I've really not been feeling all that well. I returned to Paris after my stay in the States feeling exhausted. I am just beginning to feel a little more energetic. So I've not really done any work for all these months and now find myself dried up without a single idea of what to do.

I saw the completed *Collected Poems* and think M [Mardersteig] did a very good job on that. I gather from a recent letter from Jim that he'll be bringing the lot for our signature soon and I hope you are happy with the printing. M had a lot less luck with Jim's book and is going to have to re-print....The result will be a lot less satisfactory.

I sent you a print of an etching I had not really intended to print since I messed up the plate trying to improve it. I only printed an edition to see how many decent prints I could get out of it....

Summer appears to be over now and the gray days are making their first showing with shorter daylight hours. Each year I anticipate the long spring and summer days and each year something turns up so that I can not profit from them.

Best to your mother and Laura.

Love,

Gene

Toits

Dear Gene and Ethel,

Jim called yesterday to say he had heard from you. I didn't need that as a reminder of how negligent I have been because I had known that for some months but it did nudge me into doing something to correct the negligence: RIGHT NOW! Belated thanks for the etching and for the New Year Zodiac print. They get more beautiful every year.

It has been a very long winter and though the lawns are turning green and the earliest spring bulbs are in blossom it is windy cold this morning. The sun is intermittent and I see a snowflake from time to time....

I have also been more disturbed than elated that *Life Supports* was given the American Book Award for poetry. The girls and my friends have been very excited about it and it is a kind of vindication for Jim who started to publish me when nobody else would and kept it up. And better it should happen now than thirty years ago when it might have corrupted me. Now, I have been around untouched for so long I'm like one of those corpses they display in catacombs as incorrupt. In retrospect, being left alone was very good and, I trust, good for the work and I have enjoyed the responses of readers who learned about the work privately rather than publicly. Public responders don't even have to bother with the work. There is a doctor in Houston who is a devoted reader and sent me a case of Texas grapefruit during each of the winter months. He had spent one winter in Rochester when he was an intern and felt sorry for anyone enduring a New York winter. Besides, doctors make too much money, he said, and poets don't make any.

This poet has been writing hardly at all but here is a little recent one:

Simeon's "Now"

It doesn't have to be a little child;
it can be all sorts of other things
none out of the ordinary: maybe a face,
a leaf, a certain light whirls prompts us to see
as in a mirror's blank a quality,
a presence there, a sight we abstract from it
the way from passing time we abstract what time,
destroyer of everything, doesn't touch or change:
a now, the fact of now, the all of it.

Which I send you with love
    B

Femme Couchée

49

Dear Bill,

Since Josie Whitford called to tell us the good news of the award you received I've been making false starts at letters. Nothing I write seems to say what I want to say so in despair I write this note—otherwise I'll never do so.

Ethel and I were happy to learn you had finally received some recognition outside the small circle of people who know your work. I know you have mixed feelings about his kind of recognition and I imagine I would have somewhat the same reaction if it happened to me. I don't think it would have spoiled you if you had received it much earlier. I am sure you would have given it the value it really has.

No matter how little you may think of the award it probably will have some good effects—at least in the sense you hope for. Despite all of Jim's efforts and those of your more discerning readers with such limited editions and limited outlets your work has not been able to reach all the worthwhile readers in the States and elsewhere. The award, if it does nothing else, can bring you to the attention of people who can appreciate your work but have had no means of knowing you exist. I hope.

Anyway I am so pleased for you and hope that it will mean more for you.

This has been a period of unhappy events beginning with July 1981. The less said about it, the better. I find it difficult to sort out my own feelings which are drowned in an infinite… regret and nostalgia and each day seems to add a bit more so that it is all overflowing.

Sincerely,
Gene

Seated Woman with Flowers

Eugene George Canadé

EUGENE GEORGE CANADÉ WAS BORN IN BROOKLYN, NY on November 22, 1914. He was the son of Josephine Piciulo and of the artist Vincent Canadé (1877-1961). Eugene graduated with a BA cum laude in fine arts from Brooklyn College in the City University of New York in 1939. In his youth, Eugene was in frequent contact with other known artists such as Joseph Stella, Alfred Maurer and John Flanagan, as well as his own father who was an active artist in the New York scene.

In the summers of 1938 and 1939 he received scholarships to the Cummington School of Arts in Cummington, Massachusetts. The following summer he served as assistant to Katherine Frazier, the Director of the school. During this year he set up a hand-operated typographic press to print the work of little known or beginning writers. Having purchased the press second-hand, he designed the missing parts and supervised the reconditioning of the press and its initial operation. The press was subsequently known as the Cummington Press and for several years produced books which were considered among the ten best printed books in the United States.

At Cummington in 1938 Eugene met Ethel E. Smith, from Williamsport, Pennsylvania. They were married in 1941. It was also at Cummington that the life-long friendship with the poet William Bronk began. Their friendship formed the basis for work together on several publications through the years as noted in the following bibliography.

Eugene Canadé was inducted into the armed forces in 1940 and he became a captain in the Medical Administrative corps of the US Army. Stationed in France, he was responsible for setting up a hospital in the Paris suburb of Villejuif. Upon his release in 1945, he obtained a post with the United Nations Relief and Rehabilitation Administration in Washington, DC. He began working for UNICEF in 1948 and was appointed to its Paris Office as Director of Personnel. In August 1973, the Paris Office was closed, and he took on temporary assignments in Jakarta and in Vietnam. He retired from UNICEF in 1975.

Canadé's studio in Paris

A printmaker as well as painter and sculptor, Canadé began to learn etching in the late 1930s and took up the technique again in 1977, devoting considerable attention to it. From that time to the time of his death he produced many woodcuts, some under the form of greeting cards and thematic editions on shell studies and New York bridges. His oil paintings included still life compositions and complex Cubist interpretations of shells. He also worked in wood and metal, designing and making furniture and jewelry.

Eugene Canadé's art was included in the third Exhibition of Paintings and Watercolors at the Collectors of American Art in NYC, May, 1938; in the Soldier Artist Exhibition circulated by the American Federation of Arts, October 1941 through March, 1943; and in the Salon d'Automne at the Grand Palais, Paris, France in November, 1951. He had a solo show of his work in Paris at the Lucy Krogh Gallery in December, 1963. His work was also a major part of "It Becomes Our Life: The William Bronk Collection" in the Visual Arts Gallery exhibition at SUNY Adirondack in October, 2000.

A patron of the arts and of cultural institutions, on behalf of the Canadé family he made large donations of his father's work to leading museums all over the United States. In the same capacity, he also donated a set of 19th century carving tools to the Roberson Center for the Arts and Sciences in Binghamton, NY. These tools, given to the Canadé family by the original artisan, were included in their exhibition: *Forest to Factory: The Woodworking Industries of 19th Century New York,* October 11 – December 31, 1980. He also donated a copy of George Meredity's poems with original color illustrations by his late brother, George Canadé, to the Bodleian Library in Oxford, England. On behalf of the estate of his late sister, Laura Canadé Zigrosser, he donated his and his wife's correspondence with William Bronk to Columbia University.

Throughout his life, Eugene Canadé was a man of diverse and renewed accomplishment, a vast mind whose curiosity and capacity for learning never abated. He was a generous and kind-hearted citizen of the world, beloved by his family and friends.

— Francesca Canadé Sautman

BIBLIOGRAPHY

Books with Illustrations by Eugene G. Canadé listed chronologically

Huettner, Alfred F. *Fundamentals of Embryology of the Vertebrates.* NY: Macmillan Company, 1941. [Illustrated in full, although not recognized by the author]

Blackmur, R. P. *The Second World.* Cummington, MA: Cummington Press, 1942. [Reproduces a drawing of breastplate]

Morse, Samuel French. *Time of Year: A First Book of Poems.* Introduced by Wallace Stevens. Cummington, MA: Cummington Press, 1943. [Zodiac with inscription as The Days of Man]

Bronk, William. *Light and Dark.* Ashland, MA: Origin Press, 1956. [Cover design]

Bronk, William. *Light and Dark.* New edition. New Rochelle, NY: The Elizabeth Press, 1975. [Drawing on second half-title page]

Bronk, William. *Finding Losses.* Woodcuts by Eugene G. Canadé. New Rochelle, NY: The Elizabeth Press, 1976. [Illustration on first page of text]

Weil, James L. *To Her Hand.* Warwick Press, 1977. [Original woodcut]

Bronk, William. *The Force of Desire.* With Seven Etchings by Eugene G. Canadé. New Rochelle, NY: The Elizabeth Press, 1979.

Weil, James L. *Quarrel with the Rose.* New Rochelle, NY: The Elizabeth Press, 1978. [Original etching of "Shell" from series on the theme by the artist]

Weil, James L. *Uses and Other Poems.* Etchings by Eugene G. Canadé. West Lafayette, IN: Sparrow Press, 1981.

Bronk, William. *Life Supports.* Woodcuts by Eugene G. Canadé. New Rochelle, NY: The Elizabeth Press, 1981. San Francisco: North Point Press, 1982, 1982. Jersey City, NJ: Talisman House, 1997.

Bronk, William and Eugene Canadé. Christmas Broadside Second Series #6. SUNY Buffalo; The University Library, December 1984.

"William Bronk." *Sagetrieb,* Special Issue, 7.3, Winter 1988. [Includes etching]

Bronk, William. *Selected Poems.* Selected by Henry Weinfield. NY: New Directions Books, 1995. [Includes frontispiece etching]

—Francesca Canadé Sautman

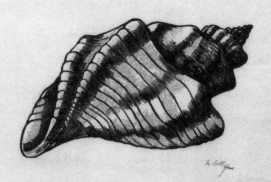

GALERIE LUCY KROHG

10 Bis, Place St-Augustin, Paris 8ᵉ - Lab. 69-78

CANADE

PEINTURES - PASTELS

6 - 21 DÉCEMBRE 1963

Poster

A TIME LINE FOR CANADÉ AND BRONK

1914   Eugene George Canadé born on November 22 in Brooklyn, NY

1918   William Bronk born on February 17 in Fort Edward, NY

1938   Bill graduated from Dartmouth University with a BA in English Literature.

1938   Eugene and Bill began their friendship at Cummington School of the Arts. Correspondence began and continued throughout their lives. Bill attended Harvard Graduate School, leaving the following year in order to write. Eugene exhibited work in the Third Exhibition of Paintings and Watercolors at the Collectors of American Art in NYC.

1939   Eugene graduated from Brooklyn College in the City University of New York with a BA cum laude in Fine Arts. In the summer he set up the Cummington Press.

1941-5 Bill served as Lieutenant in U.S.Army. He wrote *The History of the Eastern Coastal Defence* while stationed at Governor's Island. He met Eugene's father, the artist Vincent Canadé, while stationed in NYC. Eugene was a captain in the Medical Administrative Corps of the US Army, stationed in France where he helped set up a hospital in Villejuif.

1945   Eugene obtained a post with the United Nations Relief and Rehabilitation Administration in Washington, DC. Bill taught literature at Union College, Schenectady for the school year.

1946-78 Bill managed the William M. Bronk Coal and Lumber Company, Hudson Falls, NY, a business his father started in 1918.

1948-75 Eugene worked for UNICEF and moved to the Paris office as Director of Personnel. Just prior to his retirement he served assignments in Jakarta and Vietnam.

1951   Bill's first published poetry in *Origin,* edited by Cid Corman.

1956   Bill's book *Light and Dark* published by Origin Press. Eugene provided the cover design.

1975   Began their relationship with publisher James L. Weil and The Elizabeth Press with the second edition of *Light and Dark.* Canadé provided the cover design and a drawing on the second half-title page.

1976	Bill's *Finding Losses* published with woodcuts by Eugene, The Elizabeth Press.
1977	Eugene's woodcut included with James Weil's *To Her Hand,* Warwick Press.
1978	Eugene's etching "Shell" included in James Weil's *Quarrel with the Rose,* The Elizabeth Press.
1979	Bill's *Force of Desire* published with etchings by Eugene, The Elizabeth Press.
1981	Bill's *Life Supports* published by The Elizabeth Press and by North Point Press, woodcuts by Eugene. Received the National Book Award for Poetry. Eugene has etchings in *Uses and Other Poems* by James Weil, published by Sparrow Press.
1988	"William Bronk." Special Issue in *Sagetrieb*'s winter edition, includes an etching by Eugene. Bill gave a poetry reading on "Light" at The Hyde Collection in Glens Falls, NY
1995	New Directions published Bill's *Selected Poems*, edited by Henry Weinfield. This included an etching by Eugene as frontispiece.
1997	Bill had his last public reading on November 2, held at the Visual Arts Gallery in SUNY Adirondack during an exhibition of art by his friend Herman Maril.
1999	Bill died on February 22 in his home in Hudson Falls. His last poem was on the coffee table:

> Art isn't made; it's in the world almost
> unseen but found existent there. We paint,
> we score the sound in music, we write it down.

2000	October 16 – November 10. An exhibition of the art collection of William Bronk was held at SUNY Adirondack. Many of Eugene's prints, paintings and drawings are included in the Bronk Collection. Eugene came from Paris to attend the celebration. A catalogue of Bill's gift was published which included poems he had read in 1997 at his last public reading.
2001	Eugene died on September 16 in Paris, France.

Cityscape, 1994
Etching 3/35
3 x 3 7/8
WB.1999.47

Femme Couchée, 1994
Etching 33/40
3 5/8 x 2 5/8
WB.1999.48

Untitled, 1991
Etching, 35/35
3 1/2 x 2 1/2
WB.1999.48

Action Française, 1994
Etching, 1/25
3 7/8 x 5 5/8
WB.1999.50

Toits, 1991
Etching, 32/40
2 5/8 x 3 5/8
WB.1999.51

Tree, 1991
Lift ground,
aquatint 6/35
2 7/8 x 1 5/8
WB.1999.52

Toits, 1991
Etching, aquatint 9/40
1 5/8 x 2 7/8
WB.1999.53

Les Toits, 1991
Lift ground, etching
and aquatint 3/40
1 5/8 x 3
WB.1999.54

Paysage, 1991
Lift ground, etching
and aquatint 4/35
3/4 x 1 7/8
WB.1999.55

Paysage, 1991
Lift ground, etching
11/40
1 5/8 x 2 7/8
WB.1999.56

Bridge #5, 1991
Etching 9/35
2 3/8 x 2 1/8
WB.1999.57

Arches, 1991
Etching, aquatint
9/25
1 7/8 x 2 3/4
WB.1999.59

Cityscape, 1993
Etching 1/40
3 3/4 x 2 7/8
WB.1999.59

Paysage, 1993
Etching 38/40
2 5/8 x 3 5/8
WB.1999.60

Landscape, 1992
Woodcut 27/40
1 7/8 x 3 5/8
WB.1999.61

Bridge at Night, 1993
Etching 33/35
3 1/2 x 2 1/2
WB.1999.62

Toits, 1991
Etching, aquatint
33/35
2 5/8 x 2 5/8
WB.1999.63

Steeple, 1994
Etching G/G
2 3/4 x 1 11/16
WB.1999.64

Roof Tops, 1994
Etching F/H
1 1/4 x 1 5/8
WB.1999.65

*Seated Woman with
Flowers,* 1996
Etching 25/25
4 5/8 x 3 1/5
WB.1999.66

Reclining Figure, 1996
Woodcut 6/30
1 7/8 x 4 3/8
WB.1999.67

Landscape, 1994
Etching F/F
2 3/4 x 4 1/5
WB.1999.68

*Queensboro Bridge
No. 1*, 1979
Etching 30/40
3 7/8 x 5 7/8
Wb.1999.69

*Queensboro Bridge
No. 2*, 1979
Etching 28/35
4 7/8 x 5 7/8
WB.1999.70

*Queensboro Bridge
No. 3*, 1979
Etching 35/40
3 7/8 x 5 7/8
WB.1999.71

*Queensboro Bridge
No. 4*, 1979
Etching 30/40
4 1/4 x 9 3/8
WB.1999.72

Zodiac (12 framed together)
Aries (Ram), 1952
Taurus (Bull), 1959
Gemini (Twins), 1981
Cancer (Crab), 1972
Leo (Lion), 1980
Virgo (Virgin), 1971
Libra (Scales), 1983
Scorpio (Scorpion), 1966
Sagittarius (Archer), 1959
Capricorn (Goat), 1967
Aquarius (Watercarrier), 1978
Pisces (Fish), 1961
Woodcut (Cards)
WB.1999.73

Frontpiece, 1981
Woodcut 2/37
3 7/8 diameter
WB.1999.74

Shell Composition #1,
1978
Etching 8/35
2 7/8 x 1 7/8
WB.1999.75

Shell Composition #2,
1978
Etching 10/35
2 7/8 x 2
WB.1999.76

Shell Composition #3,
1978
Etching 6/35
2 5/8 x 1 7/8
WB.1999.77

Shell Composition #4,
1978
Etching 8/40
2 5/8 x 1 7/8
WB.1999.78

Shell Composition #5,
1978
Etching 8/40
2 5/8 x 1 7/8
WB.1999.79

Shell Composition #6,
1978
Etching 8/40
2 5/8 x 1 7/8
WB.1999.80

Shell Composition #7,
1978
Etching 8/40
2 7/8 x 1 7/8
WB.1999.81

Shell Composition #8,
1978
Etching 8/40
2 7/8 x 1 7/8
WB.1999.82

Shell Composition #9,
1978
Etching 8/40
2 7/8 x 1 7/8
WB.1999.83

Shell Composition #10,
1978
Etching 8/40
2 7/8 x 1 7/8
WB.1999.84

Shell Composition #11,
1978
Etching 8/40
2 7/8 x 1 7/8
WB.1999.85

Shell Composition #12,
1978
Etching 5/30
2 7/8 x 1 7/8
WB.1999.86

Shell Composition #13,
1978
Etching 14/35
2 7/8 x 1 7/8
WB.1999.87

Shell in Action, 1978
Etching 13/45
2 7/8 x 1 7/8
WB.1999.88

Woman, Snake, Sea,
1980
Woodcut 9
5 3/4 x 4 1/4
WB.1999.89

Galaxy, n.d.
Woodcut 26/32
2 7/8 x 5 3/8
WB.1999.90

Girl with Mirror, n.d.
Etching
2 1/2 x 1 5/8
WB.1999.91

Calligraphic Tree Motif,
1984
Woodcut 40/40
6 3/8 x 5 1/4
WB.1999.92

"To Her Hand" (used)
Poem by James Weil,
n.d.
Woodcut 20/30
5 1/8 x 5 5/8
WB.1999.93

"To Her Hand" (unused)
Poem by James Weil,
n.d.
Woodcut 24/25
6 3/8 x 4 3/4
WB.1999.94

Spiral Shell, n.d.
Woodcut (Card)
5 ¾ x 4 1/8
WB.1999.95

Yellow Church, n.d.
Woodcut (Card)
5 7/8 x 4 ¼
WB.1999.96

Shell Study – Black/
Brown, n.d.
Woodcut (Card)
6 x 4 3/8
WB.1999.97

Tilted Columns, n.d.
Woodcut (Card)
6 1/8 x 4 1/4
WB.1999.98

Still Life with Lemon,
1997
Woodcut (Card)
4 3/8 x 6 1/8
WB.1999.99

Sleeping Girl, 1996
Woodcut 6/30
1 7/8 x 4 3/8
WB.1999.100

Winter Vocative, n.d.
Woodcut illustration
7 3/8 x 5 7/8
WB.1999.101

Chambered Nautilus,
n.d.
Woodcut (Card)
4 x 6 1/8
WB.1999.102

Shell, n.d.
Woodcut (Card)
4 ½ x 3 3/8
WB.1999.103

Fish, n.d
Woodcut (Card)
4 1/8 x 6
WB.1999.104

Finding Losses, n.d.
Woodcut illustration
1-3/15
12 1/8 x 8 3/8
WB.1999.105

Finding Losses, n.d.
Woodcut illustration
1–3/15
12 1/8 x 8 3/8
WB.1999.106

Finding Losses, n.d.
Woodcut illustration
1–3/15
12 1/8 x 8 3/8
WB.1999.107

Finding Losses, n.d.
Woodcut illustration
1–3/15
12 1/8 x 8 3/8
WB.1999.108

*Still Life with
Eggplant*, n.d.
Conte crayon
4 ½ x 6 ¾
WB.1999.109

*Still Life with Fruit
and Shells*, 1979
Oil on canvas
14 1/2 x 24
WB.1999.110

Self Portrait, 1937
Oil on board
12 1/2 x 10
WB.1999.111

Study for a Mural,
1979
Oil on canvas
24 x 53
WB.1999.112

Canadé's studio in Paris

W. SHELDON HURST is Professor of Art History at SUNY Adirondack where he has taught and served as Director of the Visual Arts Gallery since 1994. He has served as Curator of the SUNY Adirondack Art Collection since 1998 when the William Bronk Collection was bequeathed to the college. During his tenure he has facilitated the growth of the collection; it now contains over 700 pieces of art in a variety of techniques and styles. The collection includes works by artists from the United States as well as from Japan, Czech Republic, Russia, Cuba, France, Greece, and Canada. The series of Poetry and Art publications reflects his interest in relating the fine arts and the liberal arts.